The
Neat Green Cast

by Dona R. McDuff
illustrated by Clive Scruton

Scott Foresman

Editorial Offices: Glenview, Illinois • New York, New York
Sales Offices: Reading, Massachusetts • Duluth, Georgia
Glenview, Illinois • Carrollton, Texas • Menlo Park, California

Dean and I are friends.
One time we rode our sleds.
I wanted to beat Dean.
He wanted to beat me.

We were going fast.

I tipped over.

My sled tipped over too.

"Help me!" I yelled.

"I think I broke my leg!"

I went to the doctor.
She looked at me.
She checked my right leg.

"Look," said the doctor.
"You broke your leg here.
Now we have to help it heal."

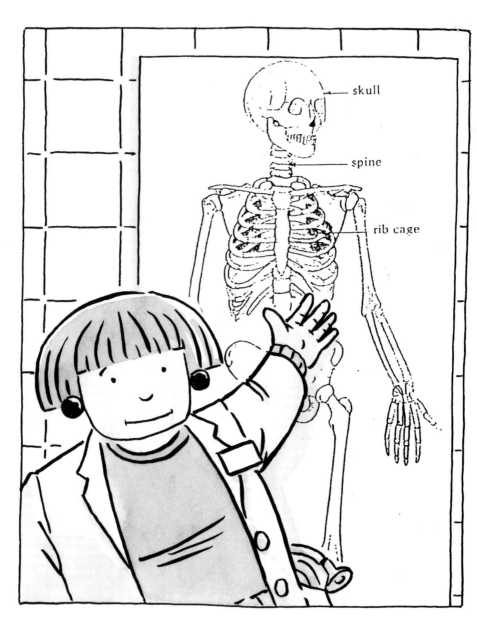

Labels on skeleton: skull, spine, rib cage

"You have 206 bones.
You broke only one of them."

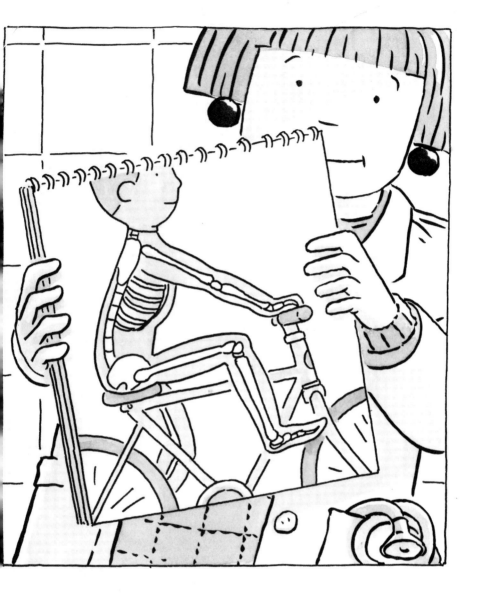

"Bones don't bend," she said.
"They help you run and play.
Bones are like a frame."

"Well," said the doctor.
"Do you want a green cast?
Or do you like blue?"
"Green is neat," I said.
"I want a green cast."

"Your leg needs to heal.
This cast will help.
I'll check it in four weeks."

"Four weeks!" I said.
"That's too long!
What will I do?"

"You look so sad," said Dad.
We'll go buy a treat."
We stopped for ice cream.

Dean was at the shop.

I sat down next to him.

"What a neat cast!" he said.

"Want to go for a sled ride?"

I laughed. "Only in our dreams!"

Phonics for Families: This book gives practice in reading words with the long *e*, spelled *ea*, as in *neat;* action words that end with the letters *ed,* as in *tipped* and *wanted*; and the high-frequency words *think, or, right, only,* and *buy.* Read the story together. Then ask your child to find all the words in the story that have long *e* spelled *ea*.

Phonics Skills: Long *e* spelled *ea;* Inflected ending *-ed* (with and without spelling change: double the final consonants)

High-Frequency Words: *think, or, right, only, buy*